Dear Debbie & [illegible]
Thanks for y[illegible]
book. You helped bring [illegible]
Margaret Turner

Lessons with Love

A teacher's classroom experiences in an elementary school 1964 to 1979

by Mary Margaret Turner

ISBN-13: 9781979067348
ISBN-10: 1979067341

Dedication

Dedicated to all the children I taught through the years

Cover Picture

The retirement community where I live, Willamette View, once offered an opportunity to residents to fulfill a lifelong dream. All they had to do was say why they had always wanted to do the activity, and enter their name in the competition. I recalled that when I was a child, I had seen a movie being made with a hot air balloon in it. Since that time, I had always had an interest in balloons and thought how much fun it would be to go up in one.

I never really expected to have an opportunity to do it. When this contest came up, however, I submitted an application form with my desire to have a balloon ride and why, even though I was already in my mid-80s. Unbelievably, they granted me my wish. Oh, my! I invited two of my grandsons to accompany me. I was so excited.

Later I painted the watercolor on the front cover of this book trying to express how it felt to be several hundred feet up in the air, floating like a cloud at sunrise on a cool summer's morning, seeing the valley from a new perspective. It really fulfilled my dreams of being high in the air and it brought so much joy to my life.

The other paintings in this book are some of the paintings I have done in the nearly 40 years since I retired.

Contents

Acknowledgements

I would like to thank all the people who inspired me to write my stories and helped me with the publication process. I could not have completed this book without their assistance. Special mention goes to Harvey Leff who was instrumental in helping me get this book published. My thanks also to those who helped with editing and organizing the text, especially my daughter-in-law Margaret Wattman-Turner, my friends Melissa New, Debbie Gage, and Arden Jewell, and my daughter Linda Townsend.

From the author

I was born in 1918 in Texas, and moved to Oregon in 1948 with my husband, who was a Methodist minister. After raising our four children, I taught elementary school in Silverton, Oregon from 1965 until I retired in 1979. I have lived at the Willamette View Retirement Community in Portland since 2001 after my husband died.

After I retired, it was my great joy to discover that I had the ability to paint, and I have enjoyed painting with watercolors ever since. As someone once told me, art adds something to your life that nothing else can. I have also spent many years doing genealogical research and recently wrote up the story of my life.

Margaret in 1975

1. Introduction

I'd like to tell you some of my experiences from when I was a teacher in an elementary school in Silverton, Oregon in the 1960s and 1970s. The children in the school offered some challenges, but more often than not, they brought many rewards. I would like to pass on some of the stories about them to give a flavor of school life at that time, and to highlight some of the interesting children and experiences that I had in the classroom.

Before moving to Silverton, I had substituted for six years in Grants Pass, teaching half time most of that period. Several times there had been stints of six weeks or more in one classroom. (One time I even substituted for my daughter Linda's 4th grade teacher for six weeks. She found it both awkward and exciting to have her mother as her teacher. I just bent over backwards not to show any favoritism.) During those years of substituting I taught first grade through ninth grade. I would agree to teach every class except music because it was beyond my ability.

Back in the 1940s in Texas, I had taught two and a half years before and after I married during World War II, up until I was expecting my first child. During that time, we were moving around a lot, but as teachers were in short supply, I got a job wherever I went. I taught: seventh grade for a half a year; then a year with a third, fourth, and fifth grades combined; a third grade for one half year; and a sixth grade for a half year.

My first degree was from McMurry College in 1941 in Abilene, Texas. That had been enough to substitute in Grants Pass, Oregon in the early 1960s, but when I wanted to return to full-time teaching after my own children were in school and in college, the State of Oregon required me to re-qualify.

Silverton's Eugene Field Elementary School allowed me to start teaching in the fall of 1965, but that summer, and each summer for the next five years, I attended the Oregon College of Education in Monmouth, Oregon for eight weeks each time. The students with children were permitted to bring their small children with them. There was a class for them during the time we were in class. My youngest son was 8 that time, and he went each day the 15 miles to Monmouth with me. He enjoyed those classes as well as the picnic lunch we shared each day. Usually we started home about 2 p.m. It was a hard time for me, but I thought it was worth the time I spent there, and an enjoyable one too, especially with Marshall along for company.

My experience at OCE was extremely useful in shaping

my ability as a teacher, and I value the training and foundation it gave me for the classroom. One of the 'tools' was so simple that I remember it yet. An older instructor said one day: "Don't waste your spits and juices!" We sat there, stunned into silence. We looked at her in shock. We were sure we had not heard correctly what she had said. She just stood, quietly smiling.

She repeated it again: "Don't waste your spits and juices!" Then she explained her words: *If you walk into a noisy classroom, don't try to make yourself heard above the noise, but stand and wait until they see you and quiet down; then talk.*

I used this so many times, and it worked every time. When children or even adults see you standing before them, silently waiting, they get the idea that you want them to take notice that they should stop talking and listen. I still laugh when I say the words to myself: "Don't waste your spits and juices!"

In Silverton I first taught third grade. At that time the school divided the children by ability. In other words, all the high ability children were in one room and on down. As a new teacher I was given the most challenging kids. The classes were small, for which I was very thankful. Later they changed the way of dividing the children to 'all abilities in each room' and even later 'mainstreamed' the special needs students into the regular class rooms.

Over the next 14 years, I taught second, third and fourth grade until I retired in 1979. The stories in this collection come from that time. We moved from Silverton to Salem in 1967 when my husband changed jobs. I didn't want to move to a new school because I really liked the school system there and the people I worked with, so I stayed at Silverton and drove the 15 miles each way for 12 more years.

Outside of the classroom things were rewarding too. One year after union negotiations were introduced, I was asked to be the negotiator for our district. I thought the man was joking when he asked me but he was not. I kept saying "No," but he won out. It turned out to be a remarkable experience for me, and good for the district as well as the teachers. God walked me through it all and it contributed to better teacher-board relations.

The next year they nominated me for the district's "Teacher of the Year". Again I was very blessed by that experience. Melvin Peterson was my principal and Bert Kleiner was the superintendent. I was to make a booklet of my life as a teacher and as a person. It was a wonderful experience to gather the testimonials together. I asked quite a few people if they would write a letter of support, everyone from parents, fellow teachers, and professionals in the community, to former students. I have included a couple of these in these pages.

Teaching for me was a very rewarding experience. I am glad for the opportunities it afforded me in getting to know people, especially the children. It was a great blessing for me. Of course there were problems and hard times but every job has those. I have just read in the novel "The Guardian's Honor" by Marta Perry a pertinent thought (p. 199): "I've learned as I've gotten older that the best way to look at the past is to sift through it for those bright moments. They'll come up shining like a bit of beach glass in the sand, and you can just let the rest slip away." So I will tell my stories about the past with that intent, just the bright moments and leave most of the struggles behind.

2. From Anger to Love

"You will have Wayne next year," my principal told me.

My heart sank as I approached the summer because when fall came, I knew I would have Wayne.

This student had been in our school only six weeks that spring but his reputation was well known. He was always in trouble on the playground.

He had been put back into the first grade when he arrived at our school the year before as he couldn't read. I knew he had thrown a chair at his male teacher even though the teacher was a large man of 6'2", weighing at least 250 pounds.

Throughout the summer I thought and prayed for Wayne. How was I to handle a child who was so angry and troubled?

The first day of school came that fall. And sure enough, the other children in my class came in from every recess, saying, "*Wayne did this*… and *Wayne did that*." Wayne seemed to be so angry at everybody. Or maybe he felt like he was battling the whole world.

One incident I remember early on was when one of the other boys in the class – Billy – came in with a new Roy

Rogers lunchbox. The next day, when Billy went to pick up his lunchbox after school, it was gone. Most of the children had left by then, and Billy had to leave and catch the bus without it. I continued to look for it.

The very next day, Wayne came to school with a new Roy Rogers lunchbox, just like Billy's but with his name printed in felt-tip on the inside. Of course I asked him where he had got it. He declared that his mother had got it for him, and his big sister had written his name in it. I didn't want to accuse him outright of taking it, thus destroying the trust I was building with him.

Inevitably, Billy's father came to talk to me about the missing lunchbox. I explained about Wayne's lunchbox with his name in it, but I told him I didn't feel I could accuse Wayne of taking Billy's. The father could have reacted in several ways. Surprisingly, he just said, "Well, maybe Wayne needs it more than my son does. I can buy him another one." I knew Billy's family was not well off, so I was quite astounded at the father's kind and generous reaction. Not many parents would have been so understanding and wise. Billy's next lunchbox had his name in it from the very first. I still think about that father and appreciate his kindness towards another child.

Within a few weeks, the other children stopped complaining about Wayne, and started to be at peace with him. Wayne was having instruction in the classroom as well as going from our room to attend special reading classes. He also had an aide working occasionally with him in the classroom. He started to make good progress after getting lots of individual help. He became so much better behaved – in the classroom and on the playground.

Wayne was also making good progress in his ability to read and in other subjects, but was still far behind the other children. The week before Christmas, he told me his family was going to move to another town during the Christmas break. Despite my worries in the summer, by December the children and I had grown very fond of Wayne, and I was very keen to help him continue his improvement. We were very sorry at the thought of him leaving us.

I knew he really did not want to move. The children in the room had accepted him, and he wasn't in trouble on the playground any more. He knew the principal by name, and of course, the principal knew Wayne. He was such a changed child from September.

As the Christmas break approached, Wayne became more and more visibly agitated. I knew he really did *not* want to move. On the last day, when the other children were working on something else, he asked—for the first time ever—if he could draw a picture. I was thrilled at his request. It was the only time he had wanted to use crayons so I said, "Yes," of course.

He got the paper and several crayon colors, and started on his drawing. But, using mostly red and black, he started hitting the paper with a slashing motion. That was all he put on that paper with crayons. Then he wrote across the top and continued down the side: *I love you, Mrs. Turner.* I had been startled at Wayne's expression of his anger at life with the vigorous slashes of crayons, but then tears came to my eyes when I read what he had written.

I always prayed for the children and the problems that came up. The wisdom to handle those problems seemed to come to me somehow.

We all said Goodbye to him on December 23rd with

regret.

But when school started again after the Christmas break, there was Wayne. They hadn't moved after all. We were so happy he was still there, but why did the family put him through such turmoil?

Then as spring break came, the family again said they were going to move. Were they crying 'Wolf' again? Wayne and the rest of us certainly hoped so. But after spring break, Wayne was gone. They had moved about 10 miles to another small town.

We all missed Wayne very much and felt so let down. Then, on the last day of school, Wayne's mother dropped him off for the day. She didn't ask or say anything but just left him for the whole day and drove off.

Everyone was so happy to see Wayne again. The words rang out with glee: "Mrs. Turner, Wayne's here, Wayne's here!" They gathered around him and hugged him with words: "Oh, Mrs. Turner, Wayne's here!"

I wondered if the other school had built on our work or if he had gone back to fighting the world, but it soon appeared that he had continued to improve.

Joy, oh joy! They had continued the work we had begun. He sat with our class and four other classes to watch a film. I got a sack lunch from our school lunchroom, and he went with us to the park for our picnic lunch, and he was as good as gold.

How I wish I knew how Wayne fared for the rest of his life. At least he felt loved and cherished by us and our school.

When I think of him now, I don't remember his anger or problems. I mainly remember his expression of love for me which almost overwhelms me to this day.

3. Accentuate the Positive

In my shadow box is a gift, remembered with a smile, and there is an interesting story behind it. The gift was a 4-inch-tall loving cup that says 'The World's Greatest Teacher'. I received it in the most surprising circumstance.

I had a little girl in the second grade that had been retained one year so she was a year older than the other children. Arlene was very good in her work, but she would miss one day a week of school. She had a little baby sister that she liked to play with, so her mother let her stay home. I was of course concerned and discussed this with the mother, without any change in Arlene's attendance.

I understood the pull of a cute baby sister but also knew she needed to attend school to achieve. In those days we had a truancy officer for our district, so I asked him to check on her.

The first time the truancy officer went, the mother let him in; he said his piece, then left. But the next time Arlene was absent, and he visited, the family didn't bother to answer the door. Finally we decided there was not any point in sending him back week after week because she was still staying at home each week to play with baby sister. As my next effort to change Arlene's pattern, I insisted that she do all the work that she had missed when she got back to school. She became very frustrated with that as it was getting a little harder for her to complete it each time she was absent.

Our school at that time had a psychologist who came one day a month to help us with severe problems. So I asked for a meeting with the principal, the nurse, and the psychologist. After I explained the problem, we went around the table offering each person an opportunity to suggest a solution. I felt that somebody should say something. But no one came up with a single idea, not even the psychologist.

With no other ideas forthcoming, I thought: how about changing tact, and being *positive* with the mother rather than using the authoritative approach we had tried up to then. I suggested that a letter be sent from the school to the mother, saying what a *good mother* she was, and how Arlene was obviously well cared for and happy in her family. I wanted to praise the mother for doing a good job and to leave out all of our criticisms. This seemed a better proposal than nothing at all. The others quickly agreed that we should try it. I was shocked that this was the only solution mentioned, and that no other possibility was put forth by the others.

With that course of action agreed on, I thought that somebody else would write the letter. But they said, *I* should write it, and then the school secretary would type it up, and I would sign it. So much for help from the professionals! So the letter was sent.

Almost immediately, we noticed an amazing change in her behavior. From then on, Arlene did not miss another day of school.

On the last day of school that year, the mother brought a small cake to me as a gift, with the loving cup on top that said "The World's Greatest Teacher."

Even when I saw Arlene's family in the store later in the summer, they all rushed up to me and surrounded me with warm greetings as they were so happy to see me again.

So you understand why I treasure that little loving cup in my shadow box, and why I still have it after being retired for 35 years. As I think of Arlene now, it brings a happy smile to my lips, and I start to sing to myself: "Accentuate the positive, eliminate the negative…".

4. The Moving Desk

I can see her yet, with red hair with lots of freckles across her nose and an impish smile on her cute face. She was a real "tomboy" type of girl. She was the middle one of three girls in her family. Her dad called her his "boy."

She was a joy to teach except for one thing. She liked to raise her feet up on her toes, so her knees lifted up the desk. She thought that was fun. That wouldn't have been too bad, except she then scooted her desk and chair forward. I had her by my desk as she was so mischievous. When I wrote something on the blackboard and then turned around, she often would be right there. I nearly fell over her once as she was right behind me. I tried different things to get her to stay in place but nothing seemed to work.

Then one day I told another teacher about it. She suggested I get a string, make a circle around her desk and chair and she would stay put. *That's a weird suggestion*, I thought. Besides, the string itself would not stay put any more than the desk and chair on our slick linoleum.

Well, I decided to try it since there was nothing else that I knew to do. But instead of string, I just drew a circle with chalk around her desk and chair.

Well, it worked! That was the end of "the moving desk

and chair." Through the years I have often thought of that chalk line. Why did it work like magic on that girl? I have always wondered.

5. Rico and Noche de Paz

This Christmas season as the carols are sung, I remember Rico from more than forty years ago.

There were very few Hispanic children in our school back then. Rico was the first and only one I had in my class. Hearing Christmas carols brings him to mind because we learned 'Silent Night' that year in Spanish.

I should say that we could still celebrate Christmas those days in school. As we teachers planned a program for the parents, we decided to sing 'Silent Night'. But to vary it, someone suggested that one of the teachers teach it in German as she spoke that language. I said I could teach it in Spanish since I had taken it in college. It was decided that the five second-grade classes would all sing it in English, then one class in German, and one in Spanish.

As I started to teach my class 'Silent Night' in Spanish, I realized I had forgotten some of the words. I asked Rico if he could help me and the next day, he proudly brought in the words from home of 'Noche de Paz'. As we practiced over the next few weeks, Rico was always at hand to help with the pronunciation and lead the singing. I could see his confidence growing through this experience. The class really enjoyed singing in another language, and the concert turned out very well. The parents were especially impressed with the class' accomplishment, and it meant a lot to Rico and his parents.

But that wasn't the last time we heard 'Noche de Paz'.

My room was at the corner of the hallways; one hallway led to the kindergarten, the first grade room, and two second grade rooms. Around the corner and down the other hall were the other three second-grade rooms.

After the noon recess as all the children came in, I always stood at that corner watching the children enter the outside door, and could see both ways down the halls. I could also look into my open door and watch the children in my room.

My class knew the routine when I was on hall duty after lunch. After playing hard, they needed to catch their breath so I asked them to put their heads on their desks each day. Then I would read to them for a rest and for listening pleasure.

The day following the Christmas break, Rico said to the class while I was still out in the hall: 'Let's put our heads down and sing "Silent Night" in Spanish, and so they did. Remarkably, Rico continued to organize the children after lunch every day after that *until the end of school in June.*

They sang ‘Noche de Paz’ every single day for the rest of the year, led by Rico. What a wonderful way to start learning to be a confident leader.

I doubt any of those children ever forgot those Spanish words, and I know that I haven’t forgotten them. I never saw Rico again after that year, but I am sure that he continued to develop his good leadership skills.

6. Older than his Years

Steven seemed older and taller than the other children in my new second grade class. However he fit in very well in the classroom without much to set him apart from the other children, except for his exceptional thoughtfulness.

If it became noisy in the hallway with our door open, Steven would get up and close it without my saying anything about it. If a window was opened to the noisy playground he would get up and close it without a sign or word from me. I would look at him and smile and often nod my head slightly so he knew he had my thanks and approval.

Whenever we had a film or a film strip (yes, we did use them back in those days), I would ask the children to put away their work to prepare for the new activity. I would get out the projector, and Steven would quietly go get the extension cord needed for it. I'm sure there wasn't another child in the room who knew where the extension cord was, but Steven did though I had never shown him where it was stored.

Throughout the year he did these things for me. I'd never had a child so helpful and considerate. At the parent-teacher conference I told his mother how thoughtful and mature he was for his years.

The next year in midwinter, while in the third grade, Steven became very ill. His family cared for him under a doctor's guidance with what they thought was intestinal flu. Late one night his condition became critical. His mother rushed him to the hospital while the father stayed home with the younger children. But Steven inexplicably died on the way to the hospital.

This was the first time any child I had taught had died. Though he wasn't in my class anymore, I still felt close to him and missed his thoughtful presence.

7. The Boy Who Lost His Shoes

As the new second graders came into my room, I knew some would be good students and some not so good, but that was to be expected.

One of the top readers was a boy named Richard, whose mother told me that she 'loved to read'. She passed her love of reading on to her son Richard. He not only loved to read but read very well too.

Richard's family was larger than most, and they seemed not to have enough money to go around. He wore the same old worn-out tennis shoes all that fall. After several weeks, and when no better shoes were on his feet, I remembered that the past spring, an almost brand new pair of tennis shoes had been left in a closet. I asked Richard if he would like to try them on. His eyes lit up as he said "Yes!"

They fit his feet well, and with a little room to grow. So he wore them home, and I put his old ones in a sack for him to take home.

Richard wore the new shoes with pride for a week or so, but there came a day when he had the old ragged ones on again.

I asked him where his new tennis shoes were.

"Well," he said, "I lost them, and mother couldn't find them."

I thought about this a while, then asked, "You were wearing them, so where did *you* put them?"

"I don't remember," he replied.

I told him: "Your mother has all the family to look after and many other things to do, like making the meals. Don't you think you are big enough to keep up with what you take off? Learn to take care of *your* things. Your mother should not have to keep up with your clothes, a boy in second grade."

Richard went home, found his shoes (outside) and learned to care for his things with pride.

I was happy to have a hand in teaching him responsibility for himself as he did not lose those shoes again all year.

8. Smart in Other Ways

Scott was a small, wiry, mischievous little boy, who always had a smile on his face. He couldn't read very well, though he had been through first and second grade and had repeated kindergarten. Now he was in third grade, and he still had trouble reading.

Early in the fall, most of the class seemed to be very tired toward the end of the school day, so I let them read library books for the last period of the day. I encouraged them to get easy ones that they could really read and enjoy. I took them one at a time to my desk to read, and looked closely at their eyes as they read. I could see that Scott's eyes didn't move together when he read. He had to wait until the other eye managed to get there, so, though he seemed to know a word on one line, he couldn't read it on the next.

I therefore told his mother she should take him to the eye doctor. As a result, she worked with him to do eye exercises to get the eyes to focus together. He still did not do well in his reading, but was good in other things like comprehension. I found out during the first year that if he sat by my desk, he would do much better in all his work. If he ever got too excited or out of line, I just had to touch his shoulder and he would settle down and do his work beautifully.

At the end of that year, I asked to move up with those same children, so they wouldn't have to change to a new teacher the next year and lose time getting acquainted with him or her. That second year, we read and read and read. I was so determined that they all should learn to read well. But alas, Scott still struggled with his reading.

Despite his difficulty, I could tell he was very intelligent. For example, he told me he'd taken a typewriter apart and put it back together. I asked him jokingly how many pieces were left over. He looked at me strangely, and said, "Not any!" It was obvious he was very capable with his hands. I smiled and told him what a wonderful job he'd done.

Once he brought a chicken foot for Show-and-Tell. It sounds disgusting, but it was quite ingenious. He showed the class how, if you pulled on the tendons which were still attached, you could get the chicken's toes to move. We related it to our body's movement.

Scott taught me that children can show their ability and intelligence in many different ways. Even those who can't read so well may be geniuses with their hands. Today he would probably be a great technician or computer expert.

9. The Letters of Condolence

Jason was a tall boy for his age in my second grade class that year. His problem was that he hadn't learned to read very well the previous year.

Fortunately, we had a new reading series that was excellent to my way of thinking. It had the children write what they read. They learned to spell the word, read the word, and write it at the same time. We even clapped the syllables of all the words. We would say and clap each of their names, which they thought was a lot of fun. I was so pleased with the progress of all the children. Even Jason started to respond well using this method.

The advanced group, for example, got to the word "identification." They didn't know the meaning of the word so I went to my closet, got out my billfold, and showed them my driver's license. We clapped the syllables, said the word, read the word in their book, then wrote the word. So by the time we had finished, the word was theirs to read and use in the future. In this way, they continually developed their vocabulary, which is why I valued the reading program so highly.

For several years I had the children write one story a week. We started on Monday and they were to finish by the end of the week. There were pictures to color that illustrated the story. The picture helped develop the story. We put new words on the board that might not be within their ability yet that they could use. The children mostly suggested the words, but I put some on the board to stretch them too. Through this activity, each child continued to advance in their abilities to read and to write at their own level. I was especially pleased to see that Jason, who had come to my class as a very poor reader, was responding remarkably well to the reading program, and was starting to progress in his reading and writing nearly as much as the others in the class.

It was in the midst of this positive atmosphere in the class, in the spring of that year, that one of the girls moved with her family to a new home her father had built. The children were sad when she left the class to go to a different school.

About two weeks before the year ended, we heard that she had suddenly been killed in a freak accident when she was hit by a truck. We were all shocked and saddened, and I knew the children would be very upset. I was particularly worried about Jason as I knew his father had worked with the girl's father in a construction firm, and that he had played with her outside of school in addition to being a friend in class.

The principal talked to me and the other teachers after the girl's death, discussing the best way to console the children. I of course wanted to talk to the children in my class about it, and we decided that it would be nice if the children could write condolence letters to the parents.

After talking with the children, they were eager to write to the girl's parents. Following our usual method, we discussed what they would write about. The words not in their vocabulary were put on the board to help them. Then they wrote the letters. I gave them plenty of time but Jason, surprisingly, finished in about twenty minutes.

I was very proud of him. He had written on both sides of the paper. Every word was spelled correctly, and capital letters and periods were all in the right places. His sentence structure was good, and he really expressed his sorrow for his friend's death. It was obvious that his genuine feelings and grief had inspired him to write a heartfelt and beautiful letter.

I was given the time off to go to her funeral, and I presented the letters to the girl's parents. They expressed their appreciation to the children, and I so hoped the letters gave the family some consolation.

10. The Wonder of J-O-E

One year, before school was out, the principal told me that Joe, a little boy of 8 or 9, would be in my second grade room that fall. Joe had repeated kindergarten, and he was older than any of the other children. His IQ was just 68, I was told. When I asked what I was to do with Joe in a classroom of second graders the principal shrugged his shoulders and said, "Whatever you can." So I read his file to get to know him as well as possible before the fall.

Those were the years after we had started main-streaming all the children and putting the special needs children into the regular class room. That is to say, we had gone from dividing the children by ability to having all abilities in a room together. I thought it was the right thing to do but how would this work out in my class room? Often a child with learning difficulties has behavioral problems as well, as I had experienced as a substitute teacher. I had the summer to think and pray, and I did *both* a lot that summer.

I had not thought of a plan of action by the start of school in the fall, even after reading all the records on Joe and talking to his teachers of the previous years. He was nearly nine years old; what was I going to do??

The first day of class arrived and there was Joe. He wasn't much taller than the other children but a little heavier. He had a beautiful smile on his face. He was dressed as well as the other children and was clean and very well behaved. He did not seem shy or ill at ease at all but was always happy to do everything the other children were doing if he could.

On the first day of school, after getting the class started on something, I gave Joe some clay to work with, the kind that doesn't harden and can be used over and over. I showed him how he could roll it between his hands or on the desk to make a long rope of it, and manipulate it in various ways. Then I took care of my duties with the other children.

Joe always seemed to be quietly and happily busy with his clay. On occasion the little girl ahead of him in the row would turn around and offer to help Joe. He took part in the class in a general way and everyone seemed to like him.

A few days later Joe said, "Look, Mrs. Turner, that's my name: J-O-E." There on his desk was his name, written with the clay using a long roll. I told him how good it was and how happy it made me to see he could write his name in clay.

A light bulb went on in my head with the thought: *If he*

can write J-O-E, he can write the ABCs. So I asked him to make all the letters, using the alphabet on the wall above the blackboard as a guide. He promptly set to work. He didn't ask me for help when he needed it, but tapped the little girl ahead of him. She would turn around to help him and then back to her work. Soon his desk was covered with the alphabet in clay. The two were so quiet about it, I didn't hear a sound. They probably had talked before and I hadn't noticed. Soon other children wanted to help Joe as well.

Of course, this wasn't the end of the story; it was just the beginning. In fact it was the best year of my teaching career, and Joe was the reason for it!

Joe learned his letters as he made them with clay, asking the girl ahead of him for help when he needed it. He learned the names and the sounds of the letters as he made them, all from his little helper-teacher. About that time, the rest of the class wanted to get in on the act. There was always someone ready and willing to help Joe. They gained confidence and reinforced their own learning through doing this.

I always felt that every child in my classroom should feel accepted, and that children should help each other. When I had previously substituted, I had observed that a teacher had let a less able student teach new classmates how to weave on a loom. It had given him so much confidence.

I read in Joe's records that in the previous years he had attended school only about two-thirds of each year. This year was different. He was gone a week when his family went deer hunting in the fall, but that was the last time that he missed a day of school After learning the sounds of the letters, he began to learn math as well. A supervisor from the county came and asked to test Joe. She had heard that he had learned his alphabet. "Yes, he knows them," I told her. After testing Joe she seemed so impressed.

About January Joe began reading the first pre-primer. He had progressed slowly but he did begin reading. It was so exciting for all of us. Each child had had a turn to help which seemed to reinforce all their learning, but most of all it made a common purpose for all to work toward.

About this time in early spring, one of the playground aids asked me one day if I knew what my children were doing during recess. No, I didn't know what my darlings were doing. There were no problems in the classroom. So……

She laughed and said there wasn't a problem, it just was something unusual; they all played as a group. Everyone together, no one was left out. Usually in second grade, boys played with boys and girls played with girls, and all the children had friends from their neighborhoods or church or wherever that they tended to play with. There were five classrooms of second graders on the playground at the same time. Playing as a class wasn't a usual thing. I'd never heard of a class so bonded that they only played with each other. The focal point of course was Joe. He was friendly, happy and very loveable, and everyone wanted to be with him.

At one point later in the year one of the most advanced students was helping Joe with math flashcards out in the hall. Joe came storming in—the only time all year he didn't have a smile on his face—and said: "Cameron called me stupid, and I'm not stupid." I replied, "Joe, you are *not* stupid. Cameron, we do not call people names. You can't help Joe anymore." The whole class heard and saw this. What a lesson for them—and they all seemed to learn it well—not to call people names. Cameron worked for months to get back into Joe's good graces, and mine too, and in time, he was again Joe's friend and helper.

By the end of the year Joe was reading the third pre-primer, not nearly as far as I had hoped but so much farther than expected at the beginning of the year. His mother or father never came to conferences, and I understood his mother could not read at all, but I assumed that his father could.

As I look back, it seems that that was the best year of my teaching: every child, no matter what their ability, got to help Joe. They were his teachers! Each one gained in self-assurance. Every one helped, and that bonded them as a group; it was the happiest of any of my classes. They learned to accept those of lesser abilities and have compassion. They learned not to call names. We were all proud of Joe's progress. I learned so much that year too.

The county supervisor came to our school again and tested Joe. She was so amazed that Joe had not only learned his alphabet, but knew sounds, and was reading. She looked at me as if I was a wonder woman. It really wasn't just me, it was my little helper-teachers too.

What did I learn from this? There are many ways of learning. Joe learned by tactile feeling, literally hands on. He internalized it by the feel. No one had ever given him this opportunity before, it seems. Or maybe it helped enough to have everyone in the classroom pulling for him. Maybe the sense of acceptance was there as never before and of course Joe attending class every day helped too. After all these years—nearly 50—I still think of Joe and the joy he brought to all of us in that classroom.

11. Greg's Letter of Recommendation

A new child came into my room during the first year of teaching in Silverton. Greg was a very sweet boy who had been in a private school in San Francisco. His mother was concerned about his being behind in my class. I promised that I would begin where he was able to do the work, and I would move him along as fast as possible.

Greg's father was overseas in Vietnam as a soldier during that war. His mother worked, so she had to drop Greg off by eight o'clock each morning. The children were not supposed to be there that early but we did not make him stay out in the cold. The teachers were to be there by eight but I was not always in my classroom as I needed to be getting ready for the day.

If I was out of the room Greg would often hide somewhere. I always knew that he was there so would talk out loud, saying, "I wonder where Greg is. I thought he was here." Then I would hear a giggle. I would go looking for him. When he came out of hiding I would give him a quick hug and talk to him a little bit. He then went to his desk or to look at things in the room. He was so quiet that it did not interfere with my work.

Some years later that group finished high school. I

remembered that I had saved some work from each of those third graders of Greg's year. When I saw the list of graduates in the local paper, I sent a congratulations card to each of them, and with it, I sent a paper of their third-grade work I had saved. Some of them called or wrote to me, or came by, and thanked me for the paper. I continued to keep up with them when I could.

A few years later when I was making a notebook of my professional life for "Teacher of the Year," I asked several people to write recommendations to add to it. Greg was in college by now, so I asked him if he would write a letter of support, which he happily agreed to do. To me it was one of the sweetest I ever received so here it is in full:

Greg's Letter

It is a pleasure to write this recommendation for Mrs. Turner. She has been one of my most outstanding teachers. She was understanding and considerate at the time I needed it most. When I was in 3rd grade, my dad was in Vietnam. Mom was worried, not knowing if he would be coming home. His discharge was overdue. I must have sensed her trouble and found myself thinking of dad all the time. Mrs. Turner was very understanding and helped me through this difficult time of life.

Mrs. Turner possesses a special uniqueness of being

able to lead a class, keep spirits up and maintain an optimistic outlook. Even after leaving grade school and going on to High School, she kept track of you. The most memorable card I received on graduation was from Mrs. Turner with papers I had done in the third grade.

In my estimation she is deserving of being nominated "Teacher of the Year" for Oregon. She would be an outstanding person to represent our state.

In Appreciation,
Gregory S.

12. Two Boys Sharing

Every year there seemed to be some children, particularly boys, in my second-grade classes who seemed quite immature. They had difficulty understanding directions or remembering what they had read. I used to have the children come to me to be taught in groups about a story, then to read the story aloud. They then had to go back to their desks and answer some comprehension questions on a worksheet about the story they had just read.

One year, two boys in particular, who didn't know each other, were in the same reading group. They often had difficulty in following directions and being able to answer the questions. They would come back individually to me after I was involved with another group and ask me repeatedly for help to complete the work. It was very disruptive to the reading group I was with, and I needed to find a solution to stop this disturbance.

I therefore sat them side by side, and told them they could discuss the questions with each other quietly, but they could only talk about the question at hand, and they were then to formulate their own answers and write them down independently. They soon were doing this successfully, and began to complete their work without needing to ask me again for help. I could see them quietly discussing the questions with each other, and coming up with answers between them.

Throughout the year, I saw them maturing and learning to work both independently and cooperatively with each other and with larger groups. They became good friends and played together on the playground. I was very happy to hear many years later that they had continued to be the closest of friends all through high school.

13. The Sister Who Gave a Birthday Party

I am saddened to hear that times have changed so much that mothers or fathers are no longer allowed to bring homemade cupcakes into school to celebrate their children's birthdays. It was always fun in my teaching days when parents came to celebrate birthdays in class, but only a small number each year would do this. It is important to note that there were some children whose parents never did this, or couldn't do this, although I was unaware of how the children might have felt about this at the time.

Until one day when the high school sister of one of my little boys stopped by and asked if she could bring some cupcakes to our school for a party for her little brother. I said yes, of course, and asked why she was willing to do this.

She replied that she had wanted *her mother* to do this while she was in elementary school, but her mother never had. I knew the mother had a number of children and probably had neither the time nor the money to bring cupcakes for a class.

The high school girl said she would make cupcakes and bring them in because she wanted to give her little brother the experience of having a class birthday celebration as she had never had.

I was impressed with the girl's good intentions and effort to give her little brother this happy experience. She said that she had got permission to be absent from her classes at the high school the afternoon of the party when she told her teachers what she wanted to do. It was such a lovely gesture, and stands out in my memory as an act of sibling love. The little brother had a wonderful party as well as the other children in the class. I remember this loving act yet.

14. Five Sticks of Gum

Earl was a boy who was on the larger side. I understood why when he said he ate six eggs one morning for breakfast. One day he came to school with a wad of gum in his mouth. I asked him if he had brought enough for all the children. When he said *no, he had not*, I let it go until reading group time when he started to read with the five sticks of gum still in his mouth.

Of course he couldn't say the words with that wad of gum. So I told him he would have to throw it away. He dramatically went to the metal waste basket near to the door. It was empty, so he thought he would get everyone's attention again by really making a loud noise with the wad of gum.

He took it out of his mouth with his right hand, drew back, and threw it hard into the empty metal basket.

But there wasn't any noise at all. He looked in the basket. No gum. Then he looked at his hand, then the basket, then his hand. He could not find the gum!

Behind him about six feet away was a round table with a girl sitting with her back to the boy. She was reading a book there. As he looked into the waste basket, then at his hand again and again, the girl behind him stopped reading.

She looked up with a startled look on her face and slowly raised a hand to her hair. Then she turned and looked at me.

I was looking at Earl, who was still trying to find the gum. I went over to him and looked in the metal wastebasket too. But then I saw the gum. The whole wad of gum had gone into the girl's hair. She looked at me with tears in her eyes. I reassured her that I would get it out.

Oh, what fun a teacher has some days!

15. Baby Brother Comes to School

During one of our second-grade units, parents would come in to talk about their profession. It helped to give the children an idea of the kinds of work adults did. With one little boy, we ended up with an unusual twist on this idea.

His family had just had a baby brother whom he was very proud of. He asked if he could bring his little brother in to show the class, and to show them how well he could take care of the baby. I agreed, and the boy came in the next day with the baby and his father. This surprised me as this was the first time a father, rather than a mother, had brought a baby in to school. However the father had been there to talk about his work so the children already knew him.

The little boy showed the baby around the class and told about looking after him. The rest of the class were very interested, and enjoyed it very much. Many of them even wished audibly that they could have a baby brother.

Then they discovered that the baby had a wet diaper. The little brother was excited to get an opportunity to show the class how he could change a diaper. We laid the baby out on a desk on his mat, and the boy proceeded to change his diaper. He very proudly took off the wet diaper and got out the new one, expertly pinning it on. It was one of the little boy's proudest days that year.

Afterward the father thanked me for allowing his son to bring in his baby brother and for realizing his dream of showing his classmates all his skills. He also said how impressed he was with my classroom technique and how well I had handled this, and how I had emphasized the learning value of the experience for the rest of the class.

The father later wrote a very nice letter about this to support my nomination for Teacher of the Year. I just remember how proud the little boy was of his baby brother and of himself that day.

Here is the father's letter:

On March 4th, 1972 a son was born and became the fifth child of the marriage of David E. G. and Carol Ann. This blessed event made all the family rejoice. As I recall, we were all at the hospital at one o'clock in the morning when Fredric was born, even mother was there. We're not so sure the doctor was really there since he walked out of the hospital half asleep.

All the children loved their new brother and each wanted to do his part in rearing the new infant. As strange as it seems, Daryll then aged seven, was just as interested as his sisters were.

Apparently, Daryll spoke of his new brother to his classmates and to his teacher, Mrs. Margaret Turner. One day in Aril 1972, Mrs. Turner invited Fredric and his dad to come to school for all the children to see a newborn child. Dad had the choice experience of presenting his new son for all the class to see. But then, Mrs. Turner, being guided by the keen insight of a good teacher, suggested that Daryll change the baby's diaper since nature had appropriately set the stage. Daryll was thrill by this choice experience, and incidentally, so was dad.

It is my personal testimony that there should be more teachers amplifying those wholesome things that make life worthwhile as was done so well that day in April 1972.

Respectfully submitted on behalf of Mrs. Margaret Turner, D.E. G.

16. Artistic and Creative Projects

Art is very important to me, and in my teaching it always played a big part in my classrooms. One of the reasons, I believe, is because I did not have any artistic stimulation myself before I was seven. I can still remember getting my first crayons at that age, and I was thrilled with all the colors and the possibilities.

When I think of all the drawing and painting of pre-school children these days, and how important parents and educators realize that is for a child's development, I know in retrospect, that I must have suffered in my personal and educational development by not experiencing creativity and artistic expression until I was seven years old.

We had just moved to California, and I had started a new school that spring when I was seven. My mother bought me a new tablet and a box of crayons, and I drew page after page of a girl in a pink dress with black patent leather shoes. In my drawings I used triangles and circles, as would a much younger child because I had no experience of drawing. In the new school, the children were finishing up a woven hammock. The teacher didn't want me to do one because I had arrived late, but I was determined (at age 7) that I wanted to weave all those lovely colors.

When I first started teaching, I wanted to put some art in every day because it so enhanced the learning situation. I think I knew that innately from my own childhood, but we now know that art helps children develop in many different ways – in their reading, in their creativity, and in all their academic work.

I often tried to use poster paint and watercolors in the classroom, for children to get experience of both. They learned colors and the use of paints, and the joy of color.

These are some of the interesting art projects I can recall:

Being Yourself

I wanted the children to realize they were individuals. To this end, I had them lie down on a large piece of butcher paper. A classmate drew around them with a pencil. Then the children painted the figure of themselves, almost always with the color of the clothes they had on that day.

For their faces, they looked at themselves in the mirror, and then painted their faces on their heads. Some produced very good likenesses of themselves. Then they cut themselves out. We stapled the figures outside the room on the wainscoting so all could see who was in our class, with the names beside each one.

A few weeks later, we made masks for the figures as Halloween was approaching. I suggested the children could made a Jack-o'-lantern head, a cat's or dog's head (with samples), or they could do something different if they had other ideas. They cut two heads out the same size, painted them whatever color they liked and stapled them together, leaving the bottom open, and place the masks on their own figure's head. They thought that was lots of fun.

A few nights later we had Parents' Night. The mothers and fathers were perhaps surprised, but then amused as they looked for their own child's figure and the mask they had made.

Christmas

At Christmas time we made a crèche scene with all the people at the Nativity. The people were made out of toilet paper tubes with papier maché heads. They were dressed with bits of cloth around the bodies and over their heads. The last morning before we were to display it, I realized we didn't have a manger for the baby Jesus. I asked one of my boys, Scott, to make a manger from some pieces of cardboard. Within ten minutes, he'd made a manger and was very pleased that it really looked like a manger.

The principal asked us to put the Nativity scene in the glass case at the front hall of the building. Everyone exclaimed over our figures.

Batiking

I read in a woman's magazine about a simplified project one could do at home, so I decided the children could do this in class. But first we had to talk about the difference between 'design', 'print', and 'picture'. So I took a day or so on each of those.

To do the batiking, we melted crayons and paraffin to extend the color by putting them in muffin tins on an electric skillet that had water in it. I tore up old sheets into rectangles of 14 x 12 inches approximately, and washed them well, and gave each child a piece of this fabric. They drew their design or picture on the fabric. Then they took a flat-tipped brush and applied the melted crayon onto the material according to their plan.

After everyone in the classroom was finished (after a week), each child crushed their cloth into a ball. I provided two buckets of dye, one black and one navy blue. With rubber gloves on, I dipped the fabric into the dye. The janitor had strung up wires across the classroom, so we hung the fabric up there to dry. The next day they were dry.

One at a time, I used an ironing board I'd brought in. The students put their fabric between a piece of paper and a paper towel, and I ironed the piece until all the wax was absorbed from the fabric and it was soft and pliable. The dye had penetrated in all the cracks where the wax had broken. The material was dyed with the waxy colors and had black or blue lines running through it. They all were so beautiful with all the colors so bright.

The pieces were then hung up as wall hangings or window hangings. The light came through those in the window as if they were stained glass. The students were very proud of their work as was I.

One boy's was just a design in the middle of the cloth. The outer part was black, but the design in the middle was so beautiful that it could have been hung in a gallery, I thought.

The year after I retired, I went to a 4th, 5th, and 6th grade school, and taught batiking to all those classes. Later one of the mothers, whom I knew, told me her son had made something with batiking for every one of his female relatives that Christmas. I was really proud that he had learned it so well he could do it on his own and make gifts for his family.

My Show and Tell

One fall I brought a sunflower from our large garden at

home. It was one of the tallest ones we had ever produced. It was 14 feet high and the flower was about 21 inches across. The janitor fastened it up to a pipe in the corner of the room and it stayed there many weeks.

We talked about the sunflower in many ways – as food, as birdseed, as an object of beauty, and as a crop. We painted sunflowers and looked at the design in the head of the sunflower.

Learning Through Cooking

Toward the end of the fourth grade, we were reading a book about pioneers in Ohio. We enjoyed reading about how the people had lived then. Towards the end of the book, we churned butter one day. The next day, I brought in yeast dough, and after they had washed their hands and desks, each of them got to knead their bread and form it into small loaves. The cooks in the cafeteria let us bake them in the ovens.

Each child got to eat his own loaf of bread and use the churned butter. I also brought a honeycomb which no child in that class had seen before. All of them took a part of their loaf of bread home because they couldn't eat it all. One boy took his loaf home, sliced it, put it on a plate with his butter, and served his family. He was so proud of it, his mother told me.

That also was the day they were allowed to dress up as pioneers—the girls in long dresses with sun bonnets; the boys in coonskin hats, etc. One boy brought a rifle that had crossed the plains on the Oregon Trail with his grandfather. I wore a long dress and a sun bonnet too. The gun had been filled with lead so it could not be shot. That day for some reason, I needed to go to the office, so I took the gun with me. The other teachers really laughed at me in my long old fashion dress and a long rifle walking down the hall.

Halloween

On Halloween we started the day before the party to make a Jack-o'-lantern from a big pumpkin. To try to gain learning from every activity, some of the children who couldn't count well to 100, got to count the seeds from our pumpkin—which were well over a hundred. Some liked to pull the squishiness out of the pumpkin along with the seeds, but others did not. But looking at the seeds was a fun thing to do, and many children counted, even those who could not count well.

We carved the pumpkin into a big Jack-o'-lantern face with a big smile on his face. When it was carved, we talked about trick-or-treating, making Jack-o'-lanterns and different things about Halloween. Then we had a party—mothers would come in and serve some cupcakes or cookies, and some juice.

I usually talked about what happened to Jack-o-Lanterns after Halloween. They knew that they were sometimes thrown about the streets and smashed up by older kids late at night. They wanted to know what we were going to do with ours. I said I was going to take it home with me and cook it, and then we were going to do something with it.

In the following days they learned many skills. First, I put the recipe for pumpkin pie on the board. Fractions were not used in the second grade but I introduced fractions so the children understood the recipe since most had never read a recipe before. I had them read it several times to learn the new words. Then they had to write the recipe down for their writing exercise.

Their next assignment was to write invitations, which we sent the principal and librarian inviting them to our pie party.

The next day, I brought back the pumpkin cooked, and with it I brought 5 pie shells with the pastry in them already. Then the fun began!

In groups of 4, they mixed the filling for the pies. One little girl mis-read salt for sugar, and nearly put a cup of salt into the mix. I stopped her just in time.

Then they poured the filling into the pie shells. Following that, we took the 5 pies to the cafeteria where we were going to bake them. The pies came out of the oven with time to cool, before the start of the pie party.

One person was to greet the principal and the librarian at the door and lead them into the room. Others had to serve the pie. We had discussed good manners and how to behave at a social gathering.

From the whole experience, the children learned a lot about cooking, about invitations and social events, and about manners, not to mention the academic value of reading, writing and fractions.

The students all wanted to take the recipe home to their mothers because they said it was the best pumpkin pie ever.

In Conclusion

Since these were still very young children, I felt it was important to emphasize that our room was their home while they were in the school. There were five second-grade classes, and it was a very large building and student body. I wanted them to feel they had a place where they felt comfortable in such a large group of people. I said that this room was like their home at school. I was "their" teacher and they were "my" children and *"their" desk was "their desk"* and no one else was to go into it. Likewise, *"My" desk was "my desk"* and they shouldn't go into it either.

I wanted every child to feel accepted by me and by every other child in the classroom. Acceptance is very important to children. And through all of these artistic and creative activities, I felt the children gained a lot. It was interesting to me that often the child that wasn't good in the academics would be good in the creative process. It is important to let children shine where they can.

17. A Poem

When I retired from Eugene Field School, one of my co-teachers wrote this poem:

Margaret

Mary Margaret, greet the sun,
Special girl to everyone.

Willing every day to share,
Ask for one, you'll get a pair.

Working hard, and all the time.
Teaching reading, math, and rhyme.

Teaching even after school.
Living by the golden rule.

Willing always, does her part.
Listens to what's in your heart.

We will miss her, oh, so much.
Her pleasant smile, her gentle touch.

Mary Margaret, greet the sun.
Special girl to everyone.

Margaret in 2012 at age 94

55795903R10044

Made in the USA
San Bernardino, CA
06 November 2017